ISBN: 9781290631242

Published by:
HardPress Publishing
8345 NW 66TH ST #2561
MIAMI FL 33166-2626

Email: info@hardpress.net
Web: http://www.hardpress.net

Singmaster
Emmeline

D 454447

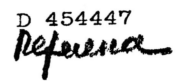

Please return this book promptly and keep it in good condition for the next borrower. *Remember* ——
YOU WILL BE THE NEXT BORROWER OF SOME OTHER BOOK!

25 '52			
eb 19 '54			
Oct 2 '64			

THE NEW YORK PUBLIC LIBRARY
CIRCULATION DEPARTMENT

CHILDREN'S ROOM
FOUR Entrance on 42nd Street   Ch

ADULT BOOKS may be kept four weeks (28 days) unless "one-week book" or "two-week book" is stamped on the flyleaf of the volume. No renewals are allowed.

CHILDREN'S BOOKS may be kept two weeks and may be renewed for an additional two weeks.

For each book kept overtime there is a fine of one cent for each day.

form 027e-ch [vl-21-50 3m]

"EMMELINE," HE SAID GENTLY, "DO YOU SUPPOSE YOU COULD HELP ME?"

EMMELINE

BY
Elsie Singmaster

With Illustrations

BOSTON AND NEW YORK
HOUGHTON MIFFLIN COMPANY
The Riverside Press Cambridge

COPYRIGHT, 1915, BY PERRY MASON COMPANY
COPYRIGHT, 1916, BY ELSIE SINGMASTER LEWARS

ALL RIGHTS RESERVED, INCLUDING THE RIGHT TO REPRODUCE
THIS BOOK OR PARTS THEREOF IN ANY FORM

TO
Miss Annie Wallace Horner
IS DEDICATED
THIS LITTLE STORY
OF HER NATIVE TOWN

CONTENTS

I. The Sound of Bugles 1
II. Emmeline and the Schmidts take a Journey 27
III. Emmeline meets the Enemies of her Country 53
IV The Second Day of Battle . . . 80
V. Private Christy says Farewell . . 103
VI. The Terror Past 130

ILLUSTRATIONS

"Emmeline," he said gently, "do you suppose you could help me?" (page 93)   *Frontispiece*

"I am in great trouble, Emmeline" . . . 32

Emmeline watched him go 128

"Yes," answered Mrs. Willing. "Bertha is asleep upstairs" 150

Reproduced by courtesy of "The Youth's Companion" from drawings by B. J. Rosenmeyer

EMMELINE

CHAPTER I

THE SOUND OF BUGLES

For an hour at least Emmeline lay quietly curled up on the rear seat of the Willing surrey. This vehicle was very old and low and broad; it had been built in the days when people made long journeys in carriages and liked to have them comfortable. At present the surrey was not in motion, but in repose in the Willing wagon shed.

Tranquillity was not characteristic of Emmeline. She was by nature a jumping jack. Although she was fifteen years old and very desirous of appearing much older, she had put few of the ways of childhood behind her.

This June day was hot, and Emmeline had been active since early morning. She had risen at six o'clock, eaten her breakfast, fed the chickens, washed the dishes, and picked the last of the red raspberries; then, while she sat by Sister Bertha's bed, she had raveled enough lint to fill a pint measure. After taking Sister Bertha her tray, she had gone downstairs to eat her own dinner hungrily. While she waited on Sister Bertha, or when she heard the neighbors talk about Sister Bertha, Emmeline's face was a blank mask. Of her sister — or, rather, her sister-in-law — Emmeline was deeply ashamed.

Sister Bertha was, alas! a rebel. She

THE SOUND OF BUGLES

had come from the South before the war had broken out to teach school in a village near Gettysburg; there young Henry Willing had seen her and had loved her, and nearly a year ago had married her. It was an act not hard to understand after you had seen Bertha. But it was war time, and between the two, in the opinion of Emmeline, there should have been undying hatred instead of love. Henry had already enlisted, and had gone away in his beautiful blue uniform to join his regiment. He cherished the comfortable conviction that his mother's home was still his, and thither he had brought his bride. To Emmeline the act was subversive of all order; it was contrary to the traditions of the world. Henry was, moreover, hers; he did not belong to this pale, dark-eyed creature to whom she had to carry trays.

To Emmeline's mother, Henry's marriage had brought great care. Soon after Bertha had come to the old home she had been taken ill with a slow fever, and had lain for weeks helpless in her bed. After a while she had got better, and had been able to walk to the window and to look out across the green fields toward the south, where two small hills lifted rounded heads above the undulating fields.

"One is called Big Round Top and one Little Round Top," Emmeline had explained in a rare moment of confidence. "There are queer rocks on Big Round Top. One is shaped like George Washington's head, hat and all, and there are two tremendous elephants, and there is Devil's Den.

THE SOUND OF BUGLES

I climbed through Devil's Den once when we went for a picnic. When we go to grandfather's you can see it. At grandfather's there is a new calf, and there is Willoughby Run, where I go fishing. I—"

At that point, Emmeline, reminding herself that she was holding commerce with an enemy of her country, had stopped.

Emmeline's mother bore cheerfully the addition to her family. Bertha was Henry's—that was reason enough; she was helpless, and she was, besides, a very lovable person. Mrs. Willing had begun bravely to make quilts for Henry's setting up in housekeeping, and even poor Bertha had tried to lift a needle in her slim, white fingers. Bertha could pick lint, but she did not succeed in sewing.

EMMELINE

Now for two weeks she had lain once more quiet and pale in her bed. Her improvement had been inspired by Henry's letters; at the coming of one she had sat up; at the coming of the second she had walked to the window. Suddenly, alas! letters had ceased to arrive, and poor Bertha rose no more. The neighbors — Mrs. Schmidt across the street, Mrs. Bannon next door — were certain that Bertha could rise if she would. Mrs. Schmidt undertook to condole with Mrs. Willing upon the difficulties of her situation. In that Mrs. Schmidt was unwise. Mrs. Schmidt's husband was a sutler in the army; and she had a great fear of his enemies.

"Ach, I pity you!" she cried in her German way. "She is strange to you and a rebel to it yet!"

THE SOUND OF BUGLES

Mrs. Willing's eyes flashed. She was a stout, able person with a great deal of common sense.

"She is my daughter-in-law, Mrs. Schmidt," she answered sharply.

Mrs. Schmidt said no more to Mrs. Willing, but to Mrs. Bannon and to Emmeline she continued to express her pity for Mrs. Willing. Emmeline made no consenting answer, but her heart was meanly pleased.

Now, lying in the old carriage, Emmeline dreamed. She had a favorite vision, in which she saw herself an army nurse, bringing comfort to hundreds of wounded Union soldiers. At the end of a long career she became engaged to a young Union general. Of course she realized that there was little chance of such dreams coming

EMMELINE

true. The war could hardly last until she was old enough to be engaged, or wise enough to be a nurse. Indeed, as a practical nurse, she had already failed. Long and irksome were the hours she spent by Sister Bertha's bed — that fact was plain even to the poor invalid herself.

It is impossible to tell to what length Emmeline's dreaming might not have gone this hot, sleepy afternoon. But Emmeline heard, or thought she heard, a sound, and to her, dreaming was far less interesting than doing. She sprang up, tossed back the long braids of her hair, and climbed down out of the carriage. Here she shook herself thoroughly awake, and thus prepared for active life, ran out into the hot sunshine.

Standing still in the garden, Em-

THE SOUND OF BUGLES

meline cocked her head. She had been certain that she heard shouting. Gettysburg, which was near the border, had often prepared itself for the arrival of the enemy, but now almost all the inhabitants except Emmeline had relinquished that fear. Emmeline still expected a battle. She went out by the side of the house and looked up and down the street, which lay bare and hot and quiet. She could hear her mother's voice as she talked in a low tone to Bertha; across the street the Schmidt baby whimpered. Emmeline, who loved babies, often took charge of the Schmidt baby.

Emmeline listened for a long minute, but heard nothing more. She shook one braid to the front of her shoulder, braided it tighter, and shook it back; then she examined the other, which proved to be still securely fastened.

Emmeline had long, thick hair and sparkling eyes. Her dress of blue and white striped calico was made with a skirt as full as a ruffle; her active legs were clothed in pantalets to match her dress; her arms and neck were bare, according to the fashion of '63. Having smoothed down her dress, Emmeline sauntered across the street, and went to the kitchen door of the Schmidt house. She realized uneasily that Bertha was crying and that her mother was trying to comfort her.

"I'll take the baby down the street, Mrs. Schmidt," Emmeline offered. "I have to go to the store."

"Thanks to you," answered Mrs. Schmidt, whose dinner dishes were still on the table. "With these six,

THE SOUND OF BUGLES

indeed, I don't know what to do, Emmy."

Emmeline took the baby with the condescending air of perfect capability to perfect incapability. She would never, she said to herself, suffer her house or her children to get into the condition in which Mrs. Schmidt's house and children were. When she had washed the baby's face and smoothed his hair, he stopped crying at once, and with a beaming smile settled himself into his little cart. Then, with "Get ups!" and with prancings, Emmeline took him through the gate and down the quiet street. At the corner she stopped to look up the hill toward the seminary building and out toward the college. Now that the boys had formed a company and had gone to war, the town

EMMELINE

and Emmeline were denied even the excitement of their presence.

Emmeline traveled more and more slowly. The air was hot and heavy. She had seen nothing that day of her bosom friend, Eliza Batterson; perhaps if she waited, Eliza might appear. Her other boon companion, Jessie Mullin, had long since been sent away from Gettysburg to visit friends in the country to the north, so much did her parents fear an invasion. Emmeline prayed that no such ignominious experience would be hers.

Presently old black Tom, who sold peanuts on the streets of Gettysburg, stopped to inquire about Henry; and then Mrs. Peter, the ever-curious, asked about Bertha. To black Tom, Emmeline gave gracious response; to Mrs. Peter, Emmeline returned an

THE SOUND OF BUGLES

answer so short and sharp as to be impertinent. Mrs. Bannon and Mrs. Schmidt were neighbors, and had a right to discuss Bertha; Mrs. Peter had none.

When Mrs. Peter had gone, Emmeline remembered uneasily that Bertha had been crying, and that there was constantly a strained, anxious look in her mother's eyes. But Henry would come back; there would probably be a letter from him in the evening mail. Not for an instant would Emmeline admit to her mind the possibility of anything else.

Presently Emmeline yawned. She could hear now unmistakably the sound of voices, but it was only the laughter of the pupils of the Young Ladies' Academy. Next year Emmeline would enter the academy; there

EMMELINE

was at present, however, between her and those young ladies a gulf as wide as the Atlantic. She nodded to them, and then took the handle of the baby cart and proceeded on her way to the village store.

But Emmeline did not reach the village store, neither then nor for a long time thereafter. She heard a new sound, and looked up. Men and women were running past her; the courthouse bell gave a single startling peal; she heard the clatter of galloping hoofs.

"What's the matter?" cried Emmeline to a passer-by. "What in the world is the matter?"

"The rebels are coming! You can see them from the corner!"

"I don't believe it!" cried Emmeline, with a throbbing heart.

THE SOUND OF BUGLES

Emmeline thought of the Schmidt baby. He was heavy, and could not be dragged, cart and all, through crowds; he would be an annoying encumbrance to a girl who liked to be in the forefront of everything. It was certainly not true that the rebels were coming; but something was coming, and Emmeline wished to be at hand to see. If she hurried up this alley and down that back street, she could reach her own yard and then the front street. She could leave the Schmidt baby, fast asleep by now, on the side porch of her house, or could thrust him, cart and all, into the kitchen.

Planning as she ran, Emmeline hurried down the alley and the back street, and at last reached her own garden. Leaving the baby in the kitchen, she came through the side yard to the gate. There she halted, with quaking knees.

It was not the rebels that had come, but some strange, tanned, half-clad creatures; they marched in good order, and looked steadily from their hollow eyes at astonished Gettysburg, which crowded, half fearful, at corners, and hung, curious, from windows. Many of the soldiers were barefooted; others wore shoes from which the soles had fallen; some had tied the soles to their shoes with strips of soiled and blackened rags. Emmeline stared with open mouth.

Half in fun and half in earnest, the strangers began to jeer at their amazed and paralyzed audience:—

"We're not a parade, Yankees!"
"We've come to eat you up!"

THE SOUND OF BUGLES

One of them caught sight of Emmeline, with her ruffled dress, staring eyes, and open mouth. "Hello, sissy!" he called. "Look out that when you close your mouth you don't bite your tongue off!"

Emmeline did not realize the full measure of the insult, for as he spoke, she had caught sight of a flag that hitherto she had beheld only in pictures — a flag that she scorned and despised. She mounted at once to a higher bar on her mother's gate.

"'Oh, say can you see, by the dawn's early light,'" sang Emmeline.

"'What so —'" Suddenly she felt some one seize her. She struggled, and cried, "Let me go! Let me go, I tell you!"

Then she realized that the hand on her shoulder was a familiar one.

"Emmeline," commanded her mother, "be still!"

"He insulted me! He's a rebel!"

"Emmeline," commanded Mrs. Willing again, "be still!" Then from her mother's lips came an incredible order: "Go and fill the water pail, and bring it here with a dipper."

"Mother!" gasped Emmeline. "Are we going to give them water?"

"Go, Emmeline!"

"They are the enemies of my country!"

"Go!" said Emmeline's mother.

When Mrs. Willing spoke in that tone, even Henry, who was a man, moved swiftly. Emmeline looked up into her mother's face, but her mother was not looking down at her. Her eyes were turned toward the street, toward that apparently unending line

THE SOUND OF BUGLES

of weariness and raggedness and burning eyes. She saw only the men's hunger, their thirst, their need.

When Emmeline returned, her mother told her to put the pail under the tree at the edge of the pavement; as she stood there waiting, with her mother's hand on her shoulder, her eyes flamed and her heart fumed. But no soldier stopped to drink.

"Go offer them water, Emmeline."

"Mother!" protested Emmeline again.

Emmeline went and filled the dipper and stood holding it out; but no soldier left the line, although the lips of many were almost black. Some looked in Emmeline's direction, some passed grimly without a glance.

"They will not drink it, mother!" cried Emmeline.

EMMELINE

"You don't end our lives that way, sissy!" jeered a passing voice.

Emmeline dropped the dipper and fled back to her mother's side. Her mother had covered her face with her hands and stood shivering. Emmeline, watching her, was for the moment awed. For the first time something of the heavy horror of war penetrated her young heart.

"We are not really going to have a battle, mother!"

Mrs. Willing shook her head. "They have come for money and supplies."

"Will they get them?"

"Not here, dear. We have n't them."

"Where will they get them?"

"At York, perhaps," her mother replied.

THE SOUND OF BUGLES

"May I go down to the square now, mother?"

With the passing of the soldiers, the feeling of horror had passed also. Emmeline felt secure here in her own quiet village.

"Why, no, of course not!" In Mrs. Willing's eyes was still that anxious, strained expression. "Where is your baby? Take him to his mother and come right back."

With a heavy heart Emmeline went to obey. She said to herself that she never could see anything; she remembered all the pleasures that had been denied her in her short life,— the political meetings and funerals she had been forbidden to attend, the parties for which she was thought too youthful,— and she felt sadly aggrieved. There was nothing to do in this dreary town. Even picnics had ceased, and home itself, devoted to the care of Sister Bertha, was home no more.

The afternoon passed, and Emmeline was sadly aware of the stir down the street. Presently, after burning a few cars on a siding, the troops went on their way. Saturday brought no excitement to brighten Emmeline's dull lot. On Sunday, when a body of Union soldiers rode through the town, Emmeline was, alas! in church. Once or twice troopers galloped through the streets, and people whispered that soldiers were riding about the fields with maps. Gettysburg was once more alert and frightened.

On Tuesday, Emmeline, sitting by the bedside of Bertha with her patchwork in her hands, heard a thrilling

THE SOUND OF BUGLES

sound — a bugle blast. Forgetting Bertha, and dropping her patchwork and workbasket, she flew to the window and stood entranced. Fate was again directing affairs in Emmeline's way. A great body of soldiers was coming down the street. They were all mounted soldiers — dusty, tanned, and weather-beaten, but well clad and well fed. Above them floated a banner that Emmeline knew, — stripes of crimson and of white, with white stars on a blue ground, like the stars of heaven, — Emmeline's flag, Henry's flag.

For almost a minute Emmeline held herself in check; then a black-slippered foot went over the window sill, and a blue-and-white-pantaletted leg followed. Sitting on the sill, she raised her voice in song.

EMMELINE

"'Glory, glory, hallelujah!'" sang Emmeline, beginning with the chorus. "'Glory, glory, hallelujah!'"

This time no one grasped Emmeline; there was no one near enough to grasp her. The soldiers cheered her, and waved to her, and saluted her. With her red cheeks, and her long braids, and her ruffled dress, she was a quaint and lovely figure. After a long time her mother called to her, and she clambered back into the room. The troops had passed, but huzzas still filled the air. Out through the town the soldiers went, and camped on Seminary Ridge.

To her keen disappointment Emmeline was not permitted to visit the camp, but from her room that night she could see the camp-fires glitter. It seemed to her that her heart would

THE SOUND OF BUGLES

burst with excitement. What would she see to-morrow? A battle?

But such good fortune could not last. When Emmeline opened her eyes the next morning, she found her mother by her bed. Mrs. Willing looked as if she had not slept.

"Get up, Emmeline," said she.

To Emmeline's dismay, she saw a little satchel in her mother's hand. Emmeline's mind was quick.

"You are not — you are not going to send me *away*, mother!"

"You are to go out to grandfather's for a little visit."

"O *mother!*" wailed Emmeline.

"Yes, Emmeline. Get up and dress. Mrs. Schmidt is going to her brother's, and you are to ride with her." Mrs. Willing was firm.

"Is there to be a battle?"

EMMELINE

"We do not know." Mrs. Willing turned away.

"O mother!" wailed Emmeline a second time.

But no "O mother!" availed. Slowly, with a bitter heart, poor Emmeline gloomily but obediently put on her striped dress.

CHAPTER II

EMMELINE AND THE SCHMIDTS TAKE A JOURNEY

MRS. SCHMIDT's brother lived on a lane that branched from the Emmitsburg Road, a mile beyond the road that led to the farm of Grandfather Willing. If Emmeline had not had to travel in Mrs. Schmidt's company, she would have been spared some of the ignominy of her departure. Not only was she going away from all excitement, all possibility of distinguishing herself, but she was journeying in Mrs. Schmidt's outrageous cart. She was accustomed to associate with the Schmidts, not as an equal, but as a superior. While she was dressing, she could see lame Mr. Bannon and Mrs. Schmidt putting the Schmidts' ancient horse between the shafts of the springless wagon. Into that wagon they had thrust already a feather bed, numerous chairs, a few of the six young Schmidts, and a quacking duck in a coop. Wildly Mrs. Schmidt flew about, frantically she commanded.

"Get the boondles, Mary! Sally, get the tarpet sack!" Thus did Mrs. Schmidt's tongue trip in its haste. "Hurry yourself, Peter!"

Emmeline wept as she braided her hair. "O mother!" she wailed again.

But her mother was not at hand to hear. With swift steps Mrs. Willing went about the house, now waiting on Bertha, now packing a luncheon for Emmeline.

In the lower hall Emmeline burst

A JOURNEY

once more into tears. Across the street the pyramid on the Schmidt wagon was growing higher and higher. Mrs. Schmidt evidently expected the utter destruction of Gettysburg. Several soldiers had come to her aid. They helped to stow her goods on the wagon; they teased her with all sorts of predictions, to which she could reply only with a feeble "Ach!"

"If the rebs get you, they'll eat you, lady!"

"Ach!" cried Mrs. Schmidt.

"Yes, sir! Now, Johnny, give me your hand and climb up here. Whoa, there!"

The soldier leaped frantically to the drooping and motionless head of Whitey.

"Ach!" cried Mrs. Schmidt. "I am a poor, poor woman!"

"Some of the rebs are looking for sweethearts, missis."

To that Mrs. Schmidt was not even able to say "Ach." She tried to explain that she was married, that she considered such a remark insulting; but before she could make her meaning plain, the soldiers had hoisted her aboard and had put the reins into her hands. Then a bright light flashed in the eyes of Mrs. Schmidt.

"Ach, Emmy, you are going with!"

To her mother Emmeline cast one more piteous glance.

"O mother," begged Emmeline earnestly, "do not make me go!"

Mrs. Willing turned from the soldier with whom she had been talking and looked down upon Emmeline. It was evident that her glance rested upon the most precious crea-

A JOURNEY

ture in the world. Her tears had fallen into the satchel that she had packed for Emmeline. It was with an anxious heart that she was sending her away. The soldier had answered her questions kindly, and had advised her to get the sick person away also; but it was impossible to get Bertha away. Then, said the soldier, she should be moved to the cellar as soon as the shooting began. Mrs. Willing, in a voice too low for Emmeline to hear, said something to the soldier, to which he answered, "God help her, lady!" Emmeline's mother was not able to suppress a groan.

"O mother," said Emmeline again, "do let me stay here!"

For answer, Emmeline's mother led her across the street and helped her to climb into the wagon.

"I am in great trouble, Emmeline," said she earnestly, "and this is the way you can help me. Go and take care of Mrs. Schmidt and the baby. Grandfather will bring you back as soon as it is safe. Pray for us all, Emmeline."

Awed by her mother's expression, Emmeline tried to gulp down her tears. As the wagon gave a preparatory jerk before getting under way, she lifted the Schmidt baby from Mrs. Schmidt's knee to her own, and was rewarded by a little brightening of her mother's face.

Mrs. Schmidt chirruped to her horse, and they were finally off. Few persons except the soldiers noticed them, for each house along the street had its own anxiety. Other horses were being harnessed, other families

"I AM IN GREAT TROUBLE, EMMELINE"

A JOURNEY

stood about in fright. Once a group of soldiers rode toward Emmeline and her friends. Their warlike appearance terrified Mrs. Schmidt.

"Now we will be killed at last!" she cried.

"We will be nothing of the kind," answered Emmeline. "Please try to drive straight, Mrs. Schmidt."

As the soldiers passed, they advised Mrs. Schmidt in a friendly way to tie her children in, at which Mrs. Schmidt at once began to crane her neck backward to count her offspring. The soldiers seemed as gay as if they were on a journey of pleasure. Riding from house to house, they rapped on the doors with their swords; their petted horses sometimes put their noses in at the windows. The soldiers ordered people to stay in their cellars. If only

EMMELINE

Emmeline could stay in a cellar — an adventure in itself unspeakably delightful.

"Ach, Emmy," cried Mrs. Schmidt, "will we ever get to your gran'pop and my brother?"

"I hope not," answered Emmeline, at which cryptic remark Mrs. Schmidt sank into silent gloom.

Just before they reached the Evergreen Cemetery, with its tall pine trees, Mrs. Schmidt turned old Whitey aside, and drove into a country road that ran between pleasant fields. Some were cultivated, and others were carpeted with daisies; on all the fences wild roses bloomed. It was now eight o'clock, and the July sun shone hotter and hotter. Mrs. Schmidt panted, and grew red in the face, and tried to fan herself with her old sunbonnet.

A JOURNEY

At any other time Emmeline would have enjoyed the excursion. Before her, but still several miles away, the two Round Tops rose against the hazy horizon. The Emmitsburg Road which they traveled lay between two long ridges of varying height, named Cemetery Ridge and Seminary Ridge. Presently they would turn to the west, and cross Seminary Ridge. Beyond it, about half a mile, lay Emmeline's grandfather's farm, where she was always welcomed with great joy, and where there was good fishing, and a little calf, and a litter of new kittens, and the companionship of a venturesome girl, Ellen Watson by name, from the next farm.

But Emmeline did not want to go to Round Top, and she did not care to see the kittens and the calf; she wanted

EMMELINE

to stay in Gettysburg. Eliza Batterson would stay, and would have a hundred boastful things to tell her. It was bitterly disappointing to be sent away. If Bertha had not been there to be taken care of she might have stayed. She agreed with Mrs. Bannon that Bertha could rise if she would.

The little Schmidts made no sound on the journey. Terrified by their mother's fright, they huddled in their various uncomfortable positions in the body of the wagon. Once Emmeline, hearing a gentle whimper, looked round, and saw that a chair had fallen upon Betsy, and that she looked out from between the rungs as if from a cage. Scrambling back to rescue her, Emmeline observed a long line of wagons like their own coming from Gettysburg.

A JOURNEY

Giving the sleeping Carl to his mother, Emmeline now took the reins herself, and in the pleasure of managing old Whitey forgot that she was an aggrieved and disappointed person. She clucked sharply to him and switched him with the reins. When all methods of hurrying his lagging gait proved futile, she proposed that she and the older children should walk, and thus relieve him for a while of their weight. Only Mrs. Schmidt remained in the cart, with Carl in her arms.

"We are emigrants," said Emmeline, forgetting her disappointment for a moment. "We are emigrants marching o'er the plains. We——"

Then Emmeline stopped, and all the little Schmidts stopped, and old Whitey lifted his head

EMMELINE

"What is that noise over there, say?" asked Mrs. Schmidt.

"Listen!" commanded Emmeline.

"What is that noise?" demanded Mrs. Schmidt in a louder tone.

"Listen!" commanded Emmeline more sharply.

Old Whitey lifted his head a little higher. Away to the north, beyond the seminary building, toward the dim line of blue hills on the horizon, there was a sharp crack! crack! crack!

"Somebody is gunning," said Mrs. Schmidt with conviction. "I wonder what they are gunning?"

"They are shooting men!" cried Emmeline excitedly. "Our soldiers are shooting down the rebels! I——"

A deeper, heavier sound crashed upon the air and interrupted Emme-

A JOURNEY

line's sentence. The first great boom of cannon lengthened into a rumble — long, low, echoing, ominous. Whitey shivered and gave a strange snort; with a cry, Mrs. Schmidt seized the reins in both hands. But Whitey would not advance.

"Get in by me, Emmy!" cried Mrs. Schmidt. "Children, get in! Emmy, get in!"

Emmeline helped the numerous little Schmidts into the wagon, and then, climbing in after them, took the reins from Mrs. Schmidt. She assured herself that there was nothing to be afraid of. The shooting, loud as it sounded, was far away.

"We will hurry, Mrs. Schmidt. We will soon be there. Get up, Whitey! Get up, I say!"

With strange, jerky motions,

EMMELINE

Whitey started; but Whitey's efforts were exerted more in an upward than a forward direction. He pranced, if the word can be used to describe a motion so stiff; he tossed his head, he snorted again. His progress became even slower than before. The heat seemed to grow each moment more intense, but the travelers did not dare to stop in the shade.

To the north there now appeared puffs of white smoke and flashes of light. The roar became continuous; before one rolling echo was more than well begun, another hollow boom had started other echoes. Mrs. Schmidt grew pale and the baby began to cry. Emmeline became impatient with the Schmidts, impatient with the dancing horse, impatient with the rough road. They had come now to a region

A JOURNEY

which had recently been drenched with heavy rains. The wheels sank deep into the mud. Several times the travelers had to dismount while Whitey pulled the wagon out of a hole. Still the booming grew heavier and the white clouds thicker; but they were far away — far beyond the seminary building.

Emmeline and her party gazed so intently in the direction of the sound that they neglected to look ahead. At a sudden turn in the road, Emmeline gave a cry and pulled at Whitey's reins, although Whitey had already stopped, paralyzed. The road before them was no longer open; it was filled from fence to fence with marching troops. To Emmeline they numbered millions. Whitey snorted again; Mrs. Schmidt and her children

EMMELINE

almost ceased to breathe. To Emmeline it seemed that she and Mrs. Schmidt and the children and the duck faced the combined armies of the world.

The approaching troops made no amused comments, as the soldiers in Gettysburg had done. They were marching swiftly; some one shouted to the travelers to get out of the way, and Mrs. Schmidt tugged first at the right rein and then at the left, thinking that if Whitey would not go in one direction, he might in the other. But vainly she tugged, and vainly she adjured her steed with weeping and with strange German exclamations. At last Emmeline had to lead him to the roadside.

A corps of soldiers marched past, tramping with even, hasty step; caissons rattled by; great cannon rumbled

A JOURNEY

along; huge wagons drawn by mules lumbered through the mud. On and on marched the thousands of men, with eyes fixed before them, as those deeper, wilder eyes of the enemy had been.

Emmeline shrank behind the broad body of Mrs. Schmidt. These were Emmeline's own soldiers, but they seemed grim and terrible. Surely they could whip all the other soldiers in the world! When they were almost past, Emmeline thought of Henry, and looked after them in dismay. Then she realized that, even if Henry had been among them, he could not have spoken to her. She suddenly began to long for the shelter of her grandfather's house.

When the corps had passed, Whitey was with difficulty restored to the road

— a horrible road, in which the ruts were now much deeper and the stones more protruding. At a snail's pace he crept. Stragglers following the soldiers passed constantly — here a man leading a string of lame horses, there a man in charge of a line of ambulances or a damaged cannon. These stragglers were not so set upon advancing that they did not have a word for Mrs. Schmidt and her children and her duck.

Finally, when the sun was almost directly overhead, Whitey stopped at the entrance of the byroad on which the elder Willings lived. Mrs. Schmidt must drive on another half mile, and then leave the Emmitsburg Road in the opposite direction. She wept at parting from Emmeline, and the children wept, and Emmeline kissed the

A JOURNEY

sleeping baby. The road was now clear; the house of Emmeline's grandparents was in sight, half a mile away.

Carrying her little satchel, Emmeline started to run. She was hungry, for she had forgotten to eat the luncheon her mother had put up for her, and she was anxious to tell her grandparents, who always listened to her with close attention, of the condition of affairs in Gettysburg. The booming sound had ceased; the battle was certainly over. Perhaps this afternoon her grandfather would drive into Gettysburg with her. That would be glorious indeed!

She opened the gate at the foot of the lane, and then, swinging it shut behind her with a slam, waved her hand toward the porch. Her grandmother knew that slam; it always brought her hurrying out to greet her darling. Emmeline hastened toward the house.

"Hello!" she called eagerly. "Where are you?"

When no one answered, she called a little louder: —

"Grandmother!"

Still there was no response. Emmeline stopped in the grassy lane, startled.

"Grandmother!" she called again. Still there was no answer. Emmeline approached the door with hesitation. Here the dog and the cat usually met her; but now no friendly animals were to be seen. Moreover, the shutters were closed and there were no familiar crocks sunning themselves on the fence.

"Grandmother!" called Emmeline again, as she put her hand on

A JOURNEY

the latch. "Grandmother, where are you?"

The latch did not yield. The door was locked! Emmeline shook it, pressed her body against it, and called again. It seemed to her suddenly that everything was mysteriously still, that the woods beyond the house were strangely dark, and that the sky was very far above her.

"Where are you?" she called. When no answer came, she ran down the slope to the barn.

The horse and the old-fashioned buggy were gone. Returning to the house, Emmeline sat down on the bench beside the door and thought.

"They are over at the Watsons'," she said aloud, with great relief. "They drove over for something. They will soon be back again."

EMMELINE

At that moment Emmeline remembered her luncheon. When she had eaten the last crumb, she felt better. She rose and started across the fields to the Watsons'. But there only deaf Grandmother Watson was at home. She had seen nothing of Emmeline's grandparents, and had evidently heard no unusual sound. Emmeline started back across the fields. It seemed to her much later than it was. Surely they would have to come back before night! The cows would have to be milked, the chickens fed. Probably they would be back by now!

Then on a rising bit of land, Emmeline stood still. The Emmitsburg Road was again filled with troops. Apparently all the armies of the world were once more gathered there; but these were new troops, marching in

A JOURNEY

the same direction as the others had gone. She could distinguish the mounted officers, the box-like caissons, the great cannon, all moving swiftly.

Across the fields drifted urgent cries. With trembling, Emmeline ran on.

But the farmhouse was still deserted. Again Emmeline tried the door. There was a window above the shed into which she could climb, but she was afraid to enter alone. Again she heard the booming of cannon. It grew heavier, more ominous.

Perhaps her grandparents had gone to the Hollingers', to the south. She could reach the Hollingers' by a circuitous route through the fields.

Again she set forth. She was now too tired to walk rapidly, and her journey consumed almost an hour. But the Hollinger house was also deserted. Too frightened to cry, Emmeline started back once more to her grandfather's farm. She was footsore and exhausted by the heat; she gasped with weariness. The heavy roaring sound of the cannon filled the air and deafened her. She remembered those fixed, staring eyes of the soldiers who had marched by.

Suddenly fear of the enemy oppressed her. She remembered stories she had heard about the cruelty in prisons, about the burning of houses, the torturing of women and children. She thought with aching heart of her mother and her home. How patiently she would sit by Bertha's bed, how obedient she would be!

Again she started to run. If the

A JOURNEY

cows were at home in the stable or the pasture, then her grandparents must surely return. But Emmeline remembered that she had seen nothing of the cows either in the stable or in the pasture! Down near the woodland the chickens had been busily scratching, but there had been no other sound or sign of animal life on the place. Perhaps the cows were down near Willoughby Run. In this great heat they would naturally have sought the shade and the cooling waters of the stream. They must surely be there!

The path lay partly in the thick woodland above the farmhouse. Coming out of it, with the farmhouse and garden immediately before her, Emmeline gave a cry of joy. The house was no longer deserted; there was a

EMMELINE

man on the porch; there was some one opening the doors of the barn.

"Grandfather!" called Emmeline. "Where have you been?"

Then Emmeline stood still. So did the man on the porch. So did other men down by the lane, by the gate, in the road. They were strangers, and there were scores of them, multitudes of them. They were soldiers in worn uniforms.

Of soldiers, as soldiers, Emmeline was not afraid; but the color of these soldiers' uniforms was gray!

CHAPTER III

EMMELINE MEETS THE ENEMIES OF HER COUNTRY

It seemed to Emmeline, as she stood at the outlet of the wood road, that an hour passed before any one spoke or moved. She herself was too much confused to speak. How had these men come up so quietly? Porch and dooryard and fields were thronged. The ridge that cut off Gettysburg from her view, the road down which she had run after she had left Mrs. Schmidt, — they, too, were filled with men, and horses, caissons, cannon, and huge wagons. And the soldiers were clad, not in friendly blue, but in hateful gray.

Only in Emmeline's immediate

neighborhood was silence. Beyond, men were shouting, horses were neighing, and wheels were creaking. Yonder, a body of troops advanced to the music of a fife; here a bugler was playing. Men were laying fires with little piles of sticks; men were going to Willoughby Run for water; men were leading horses down to drink. The throng seemed to be thickening every moment.

One man, tall and lean and brown, lifted his hand from the latch of Grandfather Willing's door and came to the edge of the porch. He had only one arm; under his coat were the bandages that still bound a recent wound. He had quiet gray eyes, which smiled at Emmeline.

He and his friends could have been to Emmeline no more startling an ap-

ENEMIES

parition than she was to them. The dust of travel had soiled somewhat her blue-and-white dress and her white stockings, but she seemed to the soldiers immaculate and fairy-like. Some exclaimed sharply; into the eyes of others came a sudden smarting and burning. In their minds they saw far away other little girls with dark braids and ruffled dresses. But Emmeline did not see their tears; these were her enemies.

The tall man with the kindly face crossed the dooryard and approached Emmeline.

"Well, sissy," he drawled, "and who may you be?"

A variety of emotions almost suffocated Emmeline. Uppermost was hatred of that particular form of address.

"I am Emmeline Willing," said she, with dignity.

Men left their piles of sticks and crowded to the fence; others, who were going on errands, made a détour in order to come a little nearer to the group.

"And who," drawled the tall man, "who may Emmyline Willing be?"

Emmeline saw the thickening crowd and remembered the dull roar that had ceased only a little while ago. She grew pale, but she answered bravely: —

"I am the granddaughter of the owner of this place."

"So-o-o! And where may the owner of this place be?"

"He has gone away." Emmeline's courage was failing. She felt the cooler air of evening and saw the shadows lengthening as the sun sank behind the woodland. "My grandfather would not wish you to be here. You ought to go away."

"Now, sissy," drawled the tall man, in a distressed voice, "don't cry!"

"I am not crying," protested Emmeline, in spite of good evidence to the contrary. "I want you to go away!"

"Well, sissy,"— the tall man seemed actually to be considering Emmeline's command,— "we could n't very well do that."

"You will have to!" cried Emmeline. "Our soldiers are here by the million! They will make you go!"

The tall man made no answer to Emmeline's assertion.

"You come here to the porch,

EMMELINE

sissy. Nobody's going to hurt a leetle gal."

"I am going home," announced Emmeline. "I am going home to my mother. The battle is over." In spite of her brave words, Emmeline moved a little nearer to the porch. "Isn't the battle over?" she said.

"Not exactly," said the tall soldier.

As he mounted the porch, the others moved away. Busy men could not stand forever looking at a little girl in a striped dress. The tall soldier laid his hand on the latch.

"Sissy, do you know any way to get this door open short of breaking it in?"

"You can't get in!" cried Emmeline. "It isn't your house! You——"

"Look here," interrupted a rough

ENEMIES

voice, "get this door open! Stop your crying and keep out of the way!"

The new comer set his shoulder against the door. The old latch held for an instant, and then, as the soldier gave another sharper thrust, the hasp tore from the wood. Emmeline grew still paler. From the porch she could see farther over the country; on hills and fields men were still marching, horses were still being led or driven, cannon and caissons were rumbling along.

The soldier who had burst open the door was now in Grandmother Willing's kitchen. He threw wide the shutters, and rattled the lids of the stove, and opened the doors of the cupboard.

Once more little Emmeline protested furiously: —

EMMELINE

"You can't touch those things!"

The soldier lifted a handful of kindling from the box by the stove, and heaping it into the fire box, lighted it.

"Can you bake?" he demanded rudely.

Emmeline did not answer. Could she bake? She had been taught here in this very kitchen, she had mixed her dough in that very bowl on the table, and had set her rising in that old-fashioned bread trough in the pantry. Would she bake? Never while breath was in her body!

Men were now crowding in at the door; an army wagon had stopped at the gate, and rough soldiers were bringing in great coffee-pots and cans. One of them brought Grandmother Willing's hens and roosters, headless,

ENEMIES

plucked, ready for the pot. Emmeline backed farther and farther into the corner, speechless and tearful.

"If I were you, I'd go upstairs, sissy," the tall man said. "Set at the window and look out. There'll be a lot going on that you can see."

Blindly Emmeline turned to obey. Crying bitterly, she climbed to her own little room, and there sat down on a chair by the window.

Where were those thousands of blue-coated soldiers? Why did they permit this great army to camp on these hills, to occupy her grandfather's house, and his fields, and the other fields round about? The enemy were now chopping down trees and tearing down fences; they had already ruined her grandfather's wheat and killed her grandmother's chickens.

EMMELINE

Why did not the blue-coated soldiers come and drive them away?

At the sound of galloping hoofs, Emmeline looked out of the window. She saw that a man on horseback had stopped at the gate and was talking with the tall soldier. His voice rose exultantly: —

"We drove 'em like sheep through the town! We have thousands of prisoners! To-morrow we'll settle them!"

"There's a leetle gal here," the tall soldier answered in his slow way. "She came to see her gran'paw, but he had gone. She lives in Gettysburg."

"She'll be safer here than in Gettysburg. Tell her to stay indoors. There'll be hotter work to-morrow."

"So they say!" drawled the tall soldier.

ENEMIES

Presently the aroma of chickens boiling in the pot began to spread through the house. It seemed to spread to an amazing distance, for from all directions men came crowding into Grandmother Willing's kitchen. The surly cook swore at them and at the stove, whereupon a drawling voice reminded him that there was "a leetle gal" within hearing. The cook's tones sank to a rumble.

But Emmeline paid no heed to the loud voices of the hungry men; she did not even smell the delicious odor of the cooking chickens. She heard only those dreadful, exultant words from the lips of the mounted soldier:—

"'We drove 'em like sheep through the town! We have thousands of prisoners! To-morrow we'll settle them!'"

EMMELINE

So that was why no Northern troops had come to her rescue and the rescue of her grandfather's house!

Emmeline ceased to cry; alarm and terror dried her tears. She thought of her mother and of Bertha. She recalled the deep earnestness of her mother's eyes.

Had there been fighting in quiet, peaceful Gettysburg? Emmeline had picked lint for padding, had wound muslin strips for bandaging, and had seen Gettysburg soldiers who had returned with a leg or an arm missing; but of actual battle Emmeline had no clear idea. She had thought of bugle blasts, of banners flying, of loud, inspiring commands; beyond that her imagination had failed. Now for the first time it became clear to her that actual danger of death threatened those whom she loved.

Where was her mother? Had Bertha been taken into the cellar as the soldier advised? Vague recollections of the details of Bertha's illness came to her, scraps of conversation between her mother and Bertha that she had heard as she passed the door of the sick room. A vague, half-formed suspicion flashed into her mind. At this moment Emmeline began suddenly to grow up. But the first speech of her adult life was childish.

"I must go home!" she cried, as she sprang from her chair.

She ran down the steps and out to the porch. Darkness had come; soldiers lay about on the grass, and the murmur of their voices spread in all directions. The moon was rising; in its

EMMELINE

first oblique rays all things looked queer and distorted.

There were many sounds: the click of pickaxes against stones, the crash of trees that were being felled, the hoarse shouts of officers giving orders. Emmeline rushed to the side of the tall soldier, who was sitting on the steps.

"I must go home!" she declared again. "I *must* go home!"

"Now you're just frightened," the tall soldier said. "There ain't no reason for you to be skeered. No harm'll come to you. We ain't wild beasts, sissy."

"I must see my mother!"

"You'll see her soon, sissy."

"My sister-in-law is sick and my brother is away." Emmeline forgot for an instant that this was an enemy of her country. "We haven't heard from him for weeks. He's in the

ENEMIES

reserves; he —" Remembering the character of her audience, Emmeline paused. Then she added, "I *must* go home!"

The tall soldier changed the subject.

"I've got a leetle gal like you; Bessie is her name — Bessie Christy. I haven't seen her for two years."

"Why not?" asked Emmeline, curious in spite of herself.

"On account of war. Now, Emmyline, 'tisn't every leetle gal can watch the sappers at work before a battle. They're the folks that build the breastworks. Look at them up there! You might see great things if you watched, 'stead of crying. You might see General Lee ride by."

"I hate him!"

"Now, sissy!"

EMMELINE

"I hate you all!"

Private Christy looked at Emmeline for a moment with a smile on his lips.

"I'll explain the army to you, Emmyline," said he. "It's a wonderful thing, an army. If you begin at the top, there's the commander-in-chief, and next below him —" Private Christy went on and on in his pleasant, drawling voice. The duty of a private was this, he explained, the duty of a sutler was that. Presently Emmeline asked him what he did. Her voice was no longer sharp; it was soft and drowsy and gentle. After a long time, when Private Christy said, "I have my work, too, Emmyline," without saying what that work was, Emmeline did not hear. Feeling a light touch on his arm, Private Christy

ENEMIES

looked down and beheld Emmeline's head resting upon it.

"Well, I vum!" said he softly.

For a long time Private Christy sat still; presently slow tears rolled down his tanned cheeks. He called to one of the men: —

"Say, you, Mallon!"

The soldier approached.

"Well, I'll be switched!" he said.

"You take her upstairs, Mallon."

It may have been that Mallon, too, had a "leetle gal" at home; at any rate, he seemed to know how to lift a sleeping person of Emmeline's size.

"The pore leetle gal!" said one-armed Christy, as he led the way.

"I'm sick of this war!" answered Private Mallon soberly.

Through the hot kitchen, where

EMMELINE

the cook had ceased his work, up the narrow stairs, they carried Emmeline to her room, and there, without waking her, laid her gently upon her bed.

"Could n't she be got out of this?" asked Private Mallon.

Private Christy shook his head. "Not nohow," said he.

Private Mallon returned to his sleep on the grass, Private Christy to his seat on the porch steps. Far away to the west there was a sudden, indefinable suggestion of a great body of men marching. Private Christy heard it and shook his head; Private Mallon nudged his neighbor.

"More coming," he said, and turned on his side.

All about on the daisies of the field lay the great carpet of sleeping men.

ENEMIES

Everyone got some sleep that night. Those who dug pits in which to lie half hidden on the morrow, or who threw up semi-circular walls of earth or timber to shelter the great cannon, gave pick and shovel after a while to others, roused from sleep, and threw themselves down near where they had been working.

Later in the night Private Christy lay down on the porch floor and slept heavily and comfortably.

Meanwhile to the rear of the great army pressed on another great army, which, being assigned its place, lay down also. The time between sunset and sunrise in early July is short enough even for those who are not exhausted by long marches.

On the ridge, officers riding back and forth in the bright moonlight marked positions and looked speculatively across at that other parallel ridge, which takes its name from the Evergreen Cemetery near one end. Far to the north, where the heavy cannonading had been, ambulances traveled the fields, guided by a whimper or a groan of pain. The greatest general of all, whom Private Christy had promised Emmeline she might see, rode about on his white horse studying the victory won, planning fresh victory for to-morrow. Thus, rapidly enough, the night waned.

When the sun rose on July 2, the thousands of soldiers in gray stirred and woke. In the Willing kitchen the surly cook began to bake his miserable biscuit; on the porch Private Christy rose and yawned, and persuaded the cook to give him place on the stove for his coffee-pot. All about in the fields and woods the thousands rose and prepared their simple breakfast. Emmeline slept and slept. Five o'clock yesterday had found her awake and dressed; but to-day five o'clock passed, then six, then seven, then eight.

Along the lines of battle all was peace; it was almost as quiet as on any other summer morning. Cannon were moved without noise under cover of the woodland, as if each great army wished to hide from the other.

Emmeline, waking, lay still and stretched out her arms. Where was she? Why was she still dressed? How had she got to bed? She sat up and looked out of the window. Then it was not a dream, after all! Round her were still the thousands of

Confederate soldiers; below her on the porch she heard Private Christy's voice.

"'Bout time to begin, ain't it?" he queried.

A voice answered that it had been time long ago. Emmeline saw the sun high in the sky; she smoothed her dress and braided her hair, and ran down the steps. There was no battle; it was the middle of the morning, and still there was no battle. Surely she could go home!

In the kitchen the surly cook gave her one of his soggy biscuits. It was nine o'clock, according to the stubby hands of Grandmother Willing's clock, which ticked on the mantel-shelf.

Emmeline's tall friend was on the porch.

ENEMIES

"Good-morning, Emmyline!" said he cheerfully.

Emmeline's war code, which she remembered clearly this morning, did not permit her to say good-morning to the enemy.

"There is no battle," she announced. "I want to go home."

"Oh, but you can't do that!"

"I must!" Emmeline looked about her. Still all was peaceful. "Just up that road! I walked almost all the way yesterday."

Private Christy shook his head.

"No, Emmyline. 'T wouldn't do."

"You are an enemy of my country!" cried Emmeline. "You have no right to keep me! I am going home!"

When Emmeline reached the gate, Private Christy called to her.

EMMELINE

"Come back, sissy!" he said.

Emmeline obeyed, weeping.

"Are n't you afraid that there biscuit 'll p'isen you?" he asked. "Seems to me if I was a woman and could bake, I could n't swallow that biscuit. You would n't bake me a real biscuit, I suppose?"

"No," answered Emmeline with decision, "I would n't."

"Well," drawled the quiet voice, "you don't have to."

Emmeline, standing with one foot on the step of the porch, considered. She had taken one bite of the biscuit. Although she was wretchedly hungry, she could eat no more.

"Will you let me go if I bake you some?" Emmeline asked.

"I'll see," answered Private Christy. The cook had left his stove, and

ENEMIES

Emmeline went to work with the familiar utensils—the yellow bowl, the wooden spoon. When the biscuits were in the oven, she looked up to find the doorway crowded with soldiers; some of them were bandaged like Private Christy; all of them were thin and deeply tanned.

"Are you going to give we-all some of them real biscuit?" asked an eager voice.

Emmeline's face flushed crimson; the position of almsgiver to her enemy was not altogether unhappy. "I'll see," she answered.

When one pan was taken from the oven, Emmeline had another ready and then another and another. Emmeline grew warmer and warmer and her cheeks rosier and rosier.

"Now," said Emmeline, "you can

EMMELINE

watch that last pan. I am going home."

"But I have n't had any!" cried Private Christy. "Nobody here knows anything about watching and turning 'em! Oh, please, sissy, bake me a pan!"

Private Christy brought in fresh fuel for the fire. A half-hour passed, another half-hour.

"Now," said Emmeline, "I am going."

Private Christy made no answer. The hungry crowd in the yard had faded away; the very atmosphere seemed charged with suspense. Emmeline looked out of the door. Was the army still here?

The army was still here; but the army was formed, massed. It was like a great animal, alive, awake, crouching for a spring.

ENEMIES

Then Emmeline screamed, and whirled round on the step. Near at hand — almost, it seemed to her, in the very house itself — the cannon roared.

CHAPTER IV

THE SECOND DAY OF BATTLE

AT the sound of the cannon shot, Private Christy, still sitting calmly on the step, looked up.

"No call to be —"

Another roar cut short Private Christy's speech. Emmeline fled into the kitchen, and Christy rose and followed her.

"No call to be skeered, sissy," he said, speaking loudly into her ear. "The shooting ain't *here*."

Emmeline covered her ears with her hands. Another fearful detonation shook the old farmhouse to its foundations. The windows trembled in their frames, the floor seemed to

SECOND DAY OF BATTLE

rock. Emmeline sank into a chair by the kitchen table, hid her face in her arms, and screamed hysterically.

"Sissy," cried Private Christy, "stop it! Don't ye dare to cry like that!" Private Christy's face was drawn. "It's an awful thing to have to hear a woman cry like that! Listen to me! The shooting ain't this way; it's that way. Them guns is half a mile off and pointing the other way. Noise can't hurt ye, don't ye know that? You've got to get used to it, for it's going to last some time. Do you hear me?" Private Christy bent his head until it was near Emmeline's. "You're the only one among all these thousands that's safe, sissy. Now stop it!"

Emmeline checked her sobs. "I can't stand it!" she cried.

"But you've got to stand it. Now

dry your tears. You can sit here, or you can go down cellar, or up attic under the eaves, or you can come out on the porch and sit with me. It ain't everyone can watch troops going into battle. I wish *I* could hold a gun again!" he added, with longing in his voice.

Thus admonished and encouraged, Emmeline rose slowly and dried her tears. Private Christy put his hand on her shoulder, and they returned to the porch.

There was little confusion to be seen. The long morning's work had put all in readiness for the engagement. Round the farmhouse regiments waited in line. Other troops had moved from their posts farther to the south, across the ridge, and down into the valley between the

SECOND DAY OF BATTLE

ridge and the two Round Tops. In that direction, and hidden from the farmhouse, were the cannon from which issued the thunderous roar. Now the sharp crack of musketry and confused shouts and yells accompanied the deep boom of the cannon. Clouds of white smoke, growing thicker every moment, rose from the valley.

Near the farmhouse, regiments waited motionless beneath their banners. Officers were already in the saddle; men stood at attention. It was as if the great commotion were no concern of theirs. But suddenly a quiver passed through them. Swords flashed in the air, commands were shouted, bugles blew; to the music of fife and drum the troops mounted the slope toward the ridge.

EMMELINE

"There they go!" cried Private Christy. "That's my company, and they're goin' without me!"

The troops topped the ridge and vanished under the white, thick blanket of smoke. As if fresh fuel had been added to a great flame, the smoke thickened, the cannonading grew heavier, the crack! crack! of musketry more incessant.

Emmeline stood with her arms clasped round the pillar of the porch. With each great detonation she grasped the pillar more tightly, as if she feared that the waves of sound might wash her away. Sometimes she closed her eyes and drew in deep breaths of air. Between her gasps of fright she stared, awed and fascinated. She saw the last troops cross the hill and the smoke clouds thicken. Pres-

SECOND DAY OF BATTLE

ently she saw black missiles hurtle through the air and bright flashes from beyond the hill divide the low-lying cloud. Suddenly she screamed. A dark object, passing over the ridge with a shrill, whistling sound, had plunged into Grandfather Willing's potato patch. Private Christy took Emmeline by the arm and led her round the corner of the house.

"Nothing but a stray shot, sissy; but if I was you, I believe I'd stay here. Nothing can hurt you through these stone walls."

He led her to a seat on the grass close to the west wall of the house. There she sat dazed. Sometimes she blinked; sometimes she smoothed absently the wrinkled, soiled fabric of her blue and white dress; otherwise she did not move. She could

EMMELINE

not think or reason; she could only listen.

Private Christy went back to his seat on the porch. Presently he returned and smiled at Emmeline, and then went into the house. There in the hot kitchen, working slowly with his single hand, he made a fresh fire, and set upon the stove Grandmother Willing's washboiler and filled it with water. Then he went upstairs and looked round. Emmeline vaguely wondered again what his business was as a member of the army. Thus far he had done nothing.

Still Emmeline sat on the grassy bank by the house. Before her was the sloping field leading to Willoughby Run. Down that field she had often raced. Under the trees by the side of the stream horses were

SECOND DAY OF BATTLE

tethered, and near by were hundreds of wagons. The sun was getting low.

Emmeline rose stiffly. It seemed to her that the roar of cannon had grown a little less thunderous. She would go round the house and out to Private Christy. Private Christy, although an enemy, was comforting. As night drew near, her longing for home grew keener, but she had begun to realize that she could not return now.

Emmeline did not find Private Christy on the porch; he was apparently running away from her. She saw his long legs carrying him up the slope; presently he broke into a run. He was not going into the battle; he was meeting those who were returning. That is, he was meeting a few — those who, although wounded, could still drag themselves along. They had left behind them thousands of their comrades, who could not join even such a halting, pitiful procession as theirs. Hundreds who had started with the procession had fallen by the way.

In the forefront of the straggling line was Private Mallon, who had carried Emmeline up to bed. His arm hung limp and his hair was clotted with blood; he fell heavily against Private Christy as they met.

Again Emmeline's arm encircled the porch pillar. In some dim, long-past existence Emmeline had dreamed of binding wounds, of smoothing fevered brows, of lifting her voice in song for the comfort of the suffering! Now Emmeline wished that the earth would open and swallow her.

SECOND DAY OF BATTLE

While she stood with her arm clasping the pillar, Private Christy and Private Mallon entered the gate. Private Christy's work was now before him; for this task had he remained with the army, while in Georgia his little Bessie grew beyond his recollection.

"Leetle Emmyline," he shouted, "you get some warm water in a basin and some old cloths, will you, Emmyline?"

Emmeline grew paler and paler; the first shocking sight of wounds seemed to paralyze her. Private Mallon, tottering in upon the arm of his comrade, fixed apologetic, tortured eyes upon her.

"It ain't no place for a leetle gal!" he muttered.

Then Emmeline took another great step toward womanhood.

EMMELINE

"I will try," she said, weeping.

When she had filled her basin with water, and had gathered the worn fragments of homespun linen that Grandmother Willing had laid away for emergencies, she took them with trembling hands into the parlor. Other wounded, blackened forms had crept in and had lain themselves down on the parlor carpet — the treasured carpet that was the pride of Grandmother Willing's life.

"Put wood in the stove, Emmyline," commanded Private Christy cheerfully, "and bring more of these rags. You'll make a fine nurse, Emmyline!"

As she turned to obey, Emmeline glanced out of the door. Creeping and crawling, the procession continued to arrive. They came through the gate

SECOND DAY OF BATTLE

one by one; they crossed the yard and the porch. A man fell heavily on the steps, and involuntarily Emmeline took her enemy by the arm and helped him up.

"I'm looking for Christy," he said in a dazed voice.

Private Christy and his work were evidently well known.

"I am to keep the boiler filled," repeated Emmeline, as she went back to the kitchen. "I am to bring warm water and towels and cloths. I am not to cry or scream. I am not to cry or scream!"

Into the house still came the wounded, into Grandmother Willing's parlor, and into Grandmother Willing's sitting-room, and up the stairs into the bedchambers, and out to the kitchen.

"Keep the kitchen clear!" commanded Private Christy. "Keep the room above clear! Nobody in there!"

Some one answered roughly that the room above was to be filled.

Private Christy's voice did not always drawl; he raised it now so that it could be heard above the slackening crash of musketry:—

"There's a leetle gal in this house, gentlemen. That is her room above the kitchen."

"A little girl!" repeated a weary voice somewhere. "I'd like to see a little girl!"

Moving about deftly, Private Christy helped this man to lie down and that one to find a more comfortable position. He seemed like a mother getting her brood together for the

SECOND DAY OF BATTLE

night; they looked up to him like children who found in him their only hope.

"Emmyline," he said gently, when she brought him the things for which he had asked, "do you suppose you could help me?"

"I could try," said Emmeline.

Private Christy passed her the end of one of the long strips of cloth.

"There, Emmyline, you take that and wind it round and round."

With a gasp, Emmeline obeyed; together she and Private Christy bound the wounded arm of Private Mallon.

The sun had vanished behind the woodland and the fleecy clouds above were golden; the cooler air of evening had begun to breathe through the old farmhouse. The sound of firing near by had ceased entirely. The battle was surely over; surely, thought Emmeline, these men would go away and Gettysburg could have peace. Perhaps she could still go home to-night! There were many wagons standing idle down by Willoughby Run; perhaps one could be spared to take her. If she could only go home and see her mother she would ask for nothing more in the world. Perhaps Henry had come back. If Henry were wounded like these men, her mother could not take care of him and Bertha, too. She *must* go home. Then Emmeline gave a great cry. Deliverance had come! She sprang to the window and began to call to some one outside. Private Christy, who was on his knees near the window, turned and looked out quickly.

SECOND DAY OF BATTLE

"They are Union soldiers!" cried Emmeline. "We have won! They will take me home! Here I am! Here I am!" She waved her arms as she called.

Private Christy looked down at the company of blue-coated soldiers. He saw what Emmeline did not see: that their progress was directed and hastened by soldiers in gray who carried muskets.

"They are prisoners, Emmyline."

"Prisoners!" cried Emmeline.

"Yes, sissy."

"Did n't we win?"

"Not exactly, Emmyline."

"What will they do with them?"

"They 'll take 'em down to that woods and guard 'em."

Leaning suddenly out of the window, Emmeline began to scream.

EMMELINE

Among the prisoners was a slender soldier to whom she called.

"There is my brother! Henry, Henry, dear, dear Henry! Here I am, Henry, here I am!"

"Be quiet, sissy!" commanded Private Christy.

Emmeline stepped across a soldier on the floor, and then across another. In frantic excitement she sought the door.

Private Christy caught and held her. "Where are you going, Emmyline?" he asked.

"I'm going to my brother."

"You don't know if it was your brother. It was too dark to see."

"It was my brother! I'm going to find him!"

"No, Emmyline."

"What will they do to him?"

SECOND DAY OF BATTLE

"Nothing."

"I haven't seen him for months and months. He is my only brother. He had a bandage round his head. Oh, please, please let me go!"

"No," said Private Christy. "Come, Emmyline, I need you."

Emmeline went back to her work, and her tears dropped on the face of the soldier by whom she knelt.

"It's too bad, sissy," said he weakly. "I wish I could help you."

Emmeline gulped back her tears. It was Henry; of that she was certain. Where had they taken him? Was he lying wounded, bleeding, alone? But Emmeline had mercifully no time for speculation. She continued to help with the bandaging and to run up and down the stairs.

About the house confusion thickened. Troops returned, powder-blackened, exhausted, famished. Many of the soldiers bound up their own wounds, or let their comrades perform that service for them. From the dark fields rose again the aroma of boiling coffee and frying bacon. The troops in the fields near at hand seemed to have moved closer together, but Emmeline did not understand the significance of the maneuver. Every few minutes she went to the window and strained her eyes into the dusk. Even in the brightening moonlight her gaze could not penetrate into the woodland where the prisoners had vanished.

Presently, when she turned from the window with a sob, Private Christy was looking down upon her. "Em-

SECOND DAY OF BATTLE

myline," said he, in his pleasant drawl, "how about them biscuit?"

"I could bake some," answered Emmeline, suddenly realizing that perhaps hunger was one of the causes of her own misery.

"Biscuits, boys!" cried one pale soldier to another. "She's going to bake biscuits!"

Feeble cheers answered.

"You won't go out of the kitchen, will you, sissy?"

"No," Emmeline promised, and went wearily down the stairs.

The joy with which her first batch of biscuits was received roused her once more. There were many who could not eat, and who called only for water. As the time passed, those cries grew louder and more frequent.

Presently, lantern in hand, a doc-

EMMELINE

tor entered and made his way from patient to patient. His clothes had dark stains upon them, and in the dim light he looked white and worn; he moved quickly from one patient to the next, as if other work awaited him. Several quiet forms he turned over, and those were presently taken away.

Emmeline baked her biscuits and spread them with apple butter from her grandmother's crocks, and carried them from room to room. There were by this time dark stains also on her striped dress. Private Christy, saying a word here, changing a position there, moved about the house like a great gray ghost.

A little later, when Private Christy found his assistant asleep by the kitchen table, he took her last pans from the

SECOND DAY OF BATTLE

oven and sat down opposite her. The night was quiet, and again there came to the ear of the listener the strange, half-defined suggestion of men marching. Private Christy ate quickly; once he interrupted his feast to go upstairs in answer to a groan. His return woke Emmeline, who lifted her head from the table and looked at him sleepily from blinking, dark-rimmed eyes.

"We've got 'em all fixed up pretty comfortable," said Private Christy softly, as if he and Emmeline had succeeded in some common task. "Now, Emmyline, it's time for you to go to bed."

"Is the battle over?" asked Emmeline.

"No, sissy."

Emmeline's mouth quivered. "Do

EMMELINE

men like to fight?" she asked, blinking drowsily.

"Like to fight?" repeated Private Christy. "Like to fight, Emmyline? Like layin' up there with arms and legs ruined? Like livin' their days without half a body? Of course they don't like it!"

"Will there be more wounds to-morrow?" asked Emmeline stupidly.

"Where there's fighting, there's wounds."

"Will it last after to-morrow?"

"God help us, no!" said Private Christy.

CHAPTER V

PRIVATE CHRISTY SAYS FAREWELL

On the morning of July 3, Emmeline got up earlier than she had on the morning of July 2. Disturbed by dreams and oppressed by the heat, she had slept restlessly. She had waked once in the night, and had gone to the window to look down upon the woods into which the Union prisoners had vanished. There, except for the stamping of restless horses, all was quiet; but beyond, toward the west, there was incessant movement. Fresh troops were arriving and were settling down for a few hours of heavy sleep. Emmeline could hear Private Christy making his rounds in the farmhouse.

EMMELINE

Now he was in the kitchen; now he brought fresh water from the pump; now he spoke soothingly to one of his comrades.

When Emmeline woke again, daylight had come, and the great host was already astir. Men laughed; even in this house of pain the soldiers were merry. Downstairs Private Christy had built a fire in the stove; Emmeline could hear the crackling flames. Stiff and sore, she rose, and, after braiding her long hair and contemplating the stained untidiness of her limp ruffles, she went down the steps. She was very tired; her mouth drooped and her eyelids seemed to have weights upon them.

Downstairs the wounded soldiers were trying to sit up; some even tried to stand. One man proclaimed

CHRISTY SAYS FAREWELL

his intention of joining his company as soon as he had eaten. Almost immediately, as if in answer to his boasting, his knees gave way and he sank to the floor.

Private Christy greeted Emmeline cheerfully: —

"Here's hot coffee for you. You look a leetle droopy. Drink this and you'll feel like a two-year-old."

Choking back her tears, which seemed to flow without any excuse, Emmeline took the cup of coffee and sat down. She lifted the cup to her lips, and then put it back into the saucer.

"I hear a noise!" she cried. "They are shooting again!"

"That's way off," answered Private Christy. "That's miles off."

"It's near Gettysburg!" Emme-

EMMELINE

line now wept outright. "I have so many troubles I can't count them all. My mother is in danger and my brother is a prisoner — I am sure it was my brother! Perhaps my home is destroyed!"

"Oh, no, sissy!"

"Can I go down to the woods to find my brother?"

"I ain't in charge of that woods, Emmyline."

"Will they take him away?"

"I don't know."

"You don't know anything!" stormed Emmeline.

Private Christy's gray eyes twinkled. It was much better to hear Emmeline storm than to have to watch her cry.

Again Emmeline made biscuit and spread apple butter and carried her

CHRISTY SAYS FAREWELL

tray about the house; again she brought water and bathed hot faces. There was nothing else for her to do. If she cast a longing glance toward the woodland, Private Christy was beside her with his "Now, Emmyline!" In the middle of the morning Private Christy called her to the door and pointed to the ridge.

"Can you see up there some mounted officers?"

"Yes."

"Do you see the white horse?"

"Yes."

"That's General Lee, Emmyline." Private Christy spoke in a solemn tone. "That's something for you to remember all your life."

"I'd rather see General Meade," said Emmeline defiantly.

"But you don't mind lookin' at

EMMELINE

my general," answered Private Christy good-naturedly.

Presently there began again another general movement of the troops about Grandfather Willing's house. They marched forward toward the ridge and passed over it, and disappeared into the valley where yesterday the cannon had roared. Now, except for the distant rumble, there was no sound.

"Where have they gone?" asked Emmeline.

"Over there," Private Christy replied noncommittally.

"What are they doing?"

"Just waiting. Now, Emmyline, you get some water for them poor souls upstairs. I have an errand to do."

When Emmeline was out of sight,

CHRISTY SAYS FAREWELL

Private Christy went down across the fields to the woodland and looked about. On the far side near the open land were the Union prisoners, well guarded. Many of them were wounded, and lay about on the ground or sat propped against the trees. In their direction Private Christy made his way. War brought about strange meetings. It was improbable but not impossible that the little girl's brother was among the prisoners.

"Goin' to pull out?" he asked a guard.

"No orders yet. I think we move with the army."

"Got a man here by the name of Willing?"

"I don't know their names."

"Can I ask?"

"No."

"Well, you find out for me, will you, Sam? His leetle sister's up here, and she thought she saw him. I suppose she could n't come down and talk to him?"

"No, she could n't."

Until eleven o'clock the distant roar continued; then followed complete silence; but the silence did not rest the ear or ease the heart. The heavy, hot atmosphere was weighted with mystery. Emmeline, moving about nervously, asked a hundred questions of Private Christy. The wounded soldiers dragged themselves to windows; from there they could see nothing except the scattered remnants of the command, the trampled fields, the ridge with its bristling cannon and its barricades. From the troops who had gone over the hill, nothing had been

CHRISTY SAYS FAREWELL

heard; it seemed as if they had been swallowed up. Emmeline made biscuit and coffee, and went to the front door and then to the attic window, and looked first toward Gettysburg and then toward Willoughby Run. She grew more and more nervous and excited.

"If it is not over, I don't understand why they don't begin! If it is over, I don't see why I cannot go home! I don't see why I have to be kept here! I don't—"

Two clear, distinct shots ended the mysterious silence. Emmeline lifted her head like a startled rabbit. It seemed that no matter how much cannonading she had heard, she could never grow accustomed to the hideous sound.

Those two clear shots were answered by all the thunders of heaven. From the ridge that Emmeline watched sped forth the fiery charge. She saw the puff of white smoke, the blinding flash, heard the great detonation. From the opposite ridge came back an equally furious answer. Then thunder and roar and blast filled the world.

Again, as yesterday, Emmeline screamed, and then at once was silent. There was no use in screaming when Private Christy across the room could not hear her, when, indeed, she could not hear herself! For hours to come Emmeline forgot her home, her mother, Sister Bertha, Henry. The terrible sound dulled her senses and paralyzed her mind.

Standing at the kitchen table, she could look through the hall and out

CHRISTY SAYS FAREWELL

of the front door. There, framed as in a picture, she saw a strange sight. A dark missile descended upon the ridge. That was no chance, stray shot, as yesterday's missile had been; it was well aimed, and it struck its mark — a caisson filled with explosives. At once caisson, horses, men, were lifted into the air. Then, a little distance away, another caisson was struck.

Soon yesterday's sad spectacle was repeated. Once more the procession of wounded crept down the slope. From the ridge to the farmhouse, and to all other farmhouses and places of refuge, — and few and scattered they were, — proceeded the wounded. No longer was the Willing farmhouse the refuge of those only who were able to walk. Thither hastened the lumbering ambulances; thither stretchers were carried; thither the wounded, supporting each other, crept inch by inch. Emmeline watched them come; Private Christy ran to help them in. In distraction Emmeline began once more to heat water and to make coffee and biscuit. That she could do! It was well that she had had yesterday's experience before to-day's!

Wounds from fragments of shell are worse than wounds from bullets; the advancing throng, alas! were wounded as terribly as they could be wounded and still live. For some, Private Christy did nothing except to help them to lie down and to cover them with one of Grandmother Willing's blankets. A doctor and a nurse, who had been assigned to the Willing

CHRISTY SAYS FAREWELL

house, tried to do the work of twenty doctors and nurses. They put Emmeline to work. They gave her hard and terrible tasks, but she accomplished them bravely, receiving an immediate reward in many blessings from those she tended. She wrote down addresses and messages, and comforted the men as best she could, and wept.

"It will make them take it easier, little girl, if you write them about me."

"Perhaps you would go to see them sometime, when the war is over."

It was amazing to hear how many had daughters or little sisters like Emmeline. As she listened to one after the other, and tried to fix their requests in her mind, her dark eyes grew wider and her face paler. Still the two hundred cannon roared. That sound unnerved even the hardened soldier and the general trained by long experience in battles, who began to ask themselves whether human spirit could endure more. The like of that sound the world had till then never heard.

In mid-afternoon came peace. As suddenly as it had begun, it seemed to Emmeline, the thunder stopped. Emmeline burst into tears, and then, not knowing that she had cried, went on with her work.

"It is over," Emmeline assured herself. "Now it is certainly over."

But Emmeline knew nothing of the tactics of war. There were still those thousands of infantry who had marched over the hill and who had as yet given no account of themselves. Where were they? They still had

CHRISTY SAYS FAREWELL

work to do. A few minutes they waited, until the last echo had died away, and then, in magnificent array, they marched forward across the fields to the opposite ridge, marched straight in the face of the enemy's cannon, which they supposed had run short of ammunition. Of those brave thousands, few returned whole across the wide fields; many did not return at all. Emmeline, watching them in the morning, had thought them wonderful; but Emmeline could not judge how glorious they were. Now they would march no more. If Emmeline had listened, she could have heard, borne upon the wind, rapturous shouts from that opposite ridge; but she heard only the broken words and gasps of the men about her. Private Christy heard with haggard, white face; the generals heard — those who survived. The greatest general of all, whom Emmeline had watched upon his white horse, listened with a breaking heart.

Gradually the clouds of smoke lifted, gradually the odor of smoke was carried away. The sun set in a stormy sky, and once more the air cooled. The battle was over; upon the wide field peace descended, but it was the peace of death and woe. From Round Top to Gettysburg and far beyond lay strewn those who a few hours before had moved in strength and pride.

Gettysburg, hearing the result of the battle, breathed a long sigh of great relief. Citizens appeared from the places where they had taken shelter; women and children came out upon the streets again, and stared at

CHRISTY SAYS FAREWELL

house walls torn by shells and at barricades thrown across streets. At Emmeline Willing's house men and women and children gazed in awe. The house had been strangely protected; it stood among its fellows unharmed. There, to Emmeline's Sister Bertha, had been sent a little child. There Bertha herself lay sleeping in the bed to which she had been restored. One by one men and women and children tiptoed into the kitchen to behold with their own eyes the little baby lying in his cradle.

Mrs. Willing moved quietly about her house and attended to her charges. All the cruelty and horror of war weighed upon Mrs. Willing. No word had come from her boy. And where was Emmeline, her darling, her little girl, whom she had un-

EMMELINE

wittingly sent into greater danger? Where were the elder Willings?

Meanwhile Emmeline worked on. She had ceased to be partisan; she asked no question either about victory or defeat. As night advanced, a great uneasiness seemed to spread. Troops were moved, trees were felled, and new breastworks erected. Emmeline's room was occupied now; a young officer lay upon the bed, and less important patients upon the floor. With his single arm, Private Christy continued to accomplish wonders.

"You are my other arm, Emmyline," he said in his drawling voice. "You must n't forget me, Emmyline."

Emmeline looked up, startled.

"Are you going away?"

"We can't stay here."

CHRISTY SAYS FAREWELL

"What shall I do, then?"

"Without *me*? Are you going to miss *me*?" said Private Christy in astonishment. "Why, you will go home, Emmyline."

"Home!" repeated Emmeline, as if the word were strange.

That night Emmeline slept on a chair by the kitchen table. Private Christy, who did not sleep at all, put a folded coat under her head and stood for a moment smoothing her dark hair; then he went on with his sad work.

Once or twice the moon showed for an instant, only to vanish; the sights upon which it looked were best shrouded in darkness. When morning dawned, troops were still massing behind the protecting breastworks. As soon as it was light, Private Christy made his way down the slope to Willoughby Run, and addressed himself once more to the soldier who guarded the prisoners:—

"Any orders?"

"Orders to be ready to move."

"Did you find Willing?"

"He's the man with his head tied up, there by the tree."

"Where's the colonel?"

"Over yonder."

Private Christy saluted the colonel and stood waiting. The colonel had a map spread out on his knee; on it he was tracing with his finger the path to the west which had been laid out for him. It was evident from the colonel's eyes that he, too, had passed a sleepless night. Presently he looked up at Private Christy, and with a nod gave him permission to speak.

CHRISTY SAYS FAREWELL

"There's a prisoner in the woods, sir, by the name of Willing. This is his grandfather's place, and his leetle sister's up there in the house. She's worked bakin' and nursin' till she's almost dead on her feet. She's a sweet leetle gal, sir. Could you leave her brother here? She's far from home and alone."

The colonel looked absently at Private Christy. Private Christy seldom asked favors; moreover, if it had not been for his self-assigned work, Private Christy might long ago have been at his home in Georgia.

"I'll see, Christy," he said, and returned to his map.

Six o'clock passed, seven o'clock, eight o'clock, and now the great wounded army seemed to breathe deeply and to turn a little and to think about rising. It was beaten, sore, but it could not pause here. It was still in the country of its enemy; it must be up and away lest worse harm befall it. Opposite lay the victor, who, although wounded also, was better furnished with the munitions of war. The beaten army must set forth on the weary way by which it had come.

All the forenoon men were marching. From the woods near by, wagons, rough, springless and uncovered, drawn by thin, jaded horses, approached over the fields to the doors of farmhouses and barns. Into them were lifted the wounded from the houses and from the open fields. They were not lifted carefully; there was not time to be careful. Across the fields toward the west to the nearest

CHRISTY SAYS FAREWELL

road the wagons went and took their places in the great line.

The skies lowered more and more, and presently from the east a chilling wind began to blow. Standing in the doorway, Emmeline felt it on her bare arms and neck, and shivered. When a wagon stopped at Grandfather Willing's door and the bearers entered, Emmeline went weeping to bid farewell to these her enemies. Private Christy had lifted his knapsack to his shoulder and had taken in his hand a staff, as if he were preparing for a long journey.

The officer in charge of the wagon ordered all men who were wounded only in the arms or head or shoulders to walk beside it; others were lifted in upon the board floors of the wagon; others were left where they lay.

EMMELINE

Emmeline clung to Private Christy's hand.

"Why don't they take them, too?" she asked.

"They're too sick, Emmyline."

"What will become of them?"

"I don't know, Emmyline. You give 'em water."

"Are you really going away from me?"

"I've got to go, Emmyline!" said Private Christy. "Marchin' orders are marchin' orders. You stay here in the house, mind! You write to me sometime, and when the war is over you've got to get acquainted with my Bessie."

"Does this end the war?" asked Emmeline.

"I don't know, sissy, but I'm afraid not. Emmyline, would you"— Pri-

CHRISTY SAYS FAREWELL

vate Christy blushed like a boy — "would you give me a kiss?"

"I will give you a dozen!" cried Emmeline.

Then, beside the lumbering wagon, Private Christy marched away. A soldier leaned on his arm before he left the porch; before he had left the gate he had given his staff to another. Bereft, Emmeline watched him go. Once he turned and nodded his head to her, and then marched on.

Private Christy looked up at the lowering sky. In a moment he felt on his cheek the first drop of the advancing torrent. Then the heavens opened on the great generals and the marching soldiers and the wounded in their open wagons.

Emmeline stood upon the step until the tall, gray figure with his wagon and his wounded had vanished in the mist. She was drenched, but she dared not go inside. She guessed why those sufferers had been left behind! And night was coming and all the world would be dark and dreadful. Emmeline could hear the ticking of Grandmother Willing's clock on the kitchen shelf and the sound of deep, anguished breathing.

Then she heard footsteps, and turned in fright. Not one of those sick men could even raise his head — who was it who came upon her so stealthily and suddenly? Through the kitchen approached a tall figure in a blue suit, with a bandaged head. Private Christy had not left his "arm" without protection.

"Henry!" cried Emmeline.

"Little Emmeline!" said Henry.

EMMELINE WATCHED HIM GO

CHRISTY SAYS FAREWELL

Into the outstretched arms flew Emmeline.

"I knew it was you! Oh, Henry, Henry, Henry!"

CHAPTER VI

THE TERROR PAST

Although Emmeline Willing's grandparents were well on in years, they were young in spirit. They liked to make excursions in their old-fashioned buggy pulled by their faithful Dandy. They had not intentionally deserted their home on the eve of battle. Grandmother Willing would have been as little likely to fly from excitement as Emmeline.

A few days before the battle Grandfather and Grandmother Willing had gone on a visit to their daughter Sally, who lived on an isolated farm to the west. Grandmother Willing had taken Tiger, the cat,

THE TERROR PAST

with her in a basket, and Rover had trotted beneath the buggy. Before they had started they had driven their two cows, Molly and Betsy, over to the Hollingers', who had promised to care for them. When the enemy had approached, the Hollingers had fled, driving their own cattle and Molly and Betsy before them.

Early on the morning of July 1 the two elder Willings bade their daughter farewell, and with no thought of what awaited them, started to return home. When Emmeline and Mrs. Schmidt were startled by the first crack of musketry, Grandfather and Grandmother Willing were even more amazed and frightened as they approached from the other direction. Suddenly soldiers appeared — it seemed to Mrs. Willing — from the

EMMELINE

ground itself, and sprang to Dandy's bridle. The soldiers turned the horse and the buggy sharply round, and Dandy dashed for the shelter of the stable he had recently left. "A battle, after all!" cried Grandfather Willing, his ruddy face paling. "A battle in Gettysburg!"

Grandmother Willing said nothing for a long time. She grasped Tiger's basket tightly with one hand and with the other clutched the side of the carriage. Tears ran down her cheeks and she drew long, gasping breaths.

"A battle in Gettysburg!" she repeated at last. "Mary is there, and Emmeline is there, and that poor young woman of Henry's is there! Like as not poor Henry is dead. What shall we do?"

"There is only one thing we can

THE TERROR PAST

do, mother; that is go back to Sally's. The town will be protected."

"I want to go home!" sobbed Grandmother Willing, much as Emmeline had sobbed. "They might get out as far as our house, and they might do damage."

"The fighting is three miles from our house, mother."

When they reached their daughter's farm, Sally came running to meet them.

"Oh, I have been so worried about you! Get down, mother. Come in. Oh, this dreadful noise! Look, father!"

Old Mr. Willing's eyes followed her pointing finger. On the main road, a few rods from the farmhouse, thousands of soldiers were marching rapidly toward Gettysburg. Their line extended back for at least a mile.

From the porch and windows of the farmhouse terrified faces watched them.

Grandmother Willing wept again.

"Perhaps our dear Henry is among them!"

"Henry, mother! Why, these are the rebels!"

"Oh, dear, Oh, dear!" wailed Grandmother Willing. "What shall we do?"

"We will do two things, mother," answered Grandfather Willing solemnly. "We will wait and we will pray."

A hill shut out from the farmhouse a view of the first day's battlefield. When Grandfather Willing and his son-in-law proposed to make their way to higher ground, such a loud outcry rose from the

THE TERROR PAST

women and children that they abandoned the plan. Gathering the family about him, Grandfather Willing prayed that the engagement might be short and victorious for the arms of righteousness. When toward evening the noise of battle ceased, grandfather hoped that his prayers had been answered.

On Wednesday morning Grandmother Willing rose early from her bed. Toward the southwest she could see the Round Tops; before her the plain was clear and beautiful. Her heart rejoiced.

"Look, father, now we can go home!"

Grandfather Willing came to the window and looked out. He saw the clear, beautiful plain, but he saw also another and a startling sight. From the west approached fresh troops. The main road, where it left the woodland, was crowded. Rapidly the throng drew near; officers shouted, drivers urged their horses, wagons rattled.

"Is there going to be *more?*" asked Grandmother Willing.

All morning the family in the farmhouse watched the road and the distant plain. The troops vanished from sight as they approached Gettysburg. When by noon there had been no further sound of shooting, Grandmother Willing suggested that they start.

"We can surely go now, father!"

Just then a boy came from a farm a mile across the fields with news that made Grandmother Willing change her mind. There had been yesterday,

THE TERROR PAST

he said, a terrible battle; Gettysburg was now in the possession of the Confederates. Troops were gathering from all directions; there was going to be worse fighting before the day was over.

It was not until late afternoon that the firing on the second day began. Then it was that Emmeline, in her grandmother's kitchen, had first screamed and whirled round and that Private Christy had told her to be still. To the watchers at the farmhouse on the hillside the time passed more slowly than it did to Emmeline. From the upper windows they could see the clouds of smoke, and could tell exactly where the cannon stood; it was clear to the Willings that the battle raged near their house.

On Friday, the third day of battle,

EMMELINE

Grandmother Willing made no request to be taken home. She woke to the sound of cannon, dull and distant; she listened with blanched face until noon. At one o'clock, when it began once more in its final and most terrible fury, Grandmother Willing covered her ears, so that she might hear less and pray more. From hundreds of terrified hearts in Gettysburg and round Gettysburg rose petitions for relief from the torture of the sound.

When silence finally came, the family on the hillside did not dare to rejoice, but waited fearfully for another roar.

But no roar came. Twilight faded to dusk, dusk to night, and silence persisted. From the direction of Gettysburg came no sound. If troops

THE TERROR PAST

moved on the Cashtown Road, the Willing family did not know. They slept heavily and woke later than was their custom. When they rose, the bright sun of other mornings was not shining. The day was cloudy, the air heavy. In the direction of Gettysburg all was dim and hazy.

"And now," said Grandmother Willing, "we can go home."

Grandfather was as patient as Private Christy. He shook his head with a gentle "No, mother." Between them and home lay thousands of troops; until they departed silence signified nothing.

All the morning the clouds thickened and the air grew heavier. At noon horsemen, riding toward the west, appeared on the main road. At the first crossroad they turned toward the south.

EMMELINE

They rode slowly, with bent heads, on tired horses. Presently wagons followed. Then to the ears of the little family on the hillside there rose from that unending line of rough ambulances a strange sound. The women and children could not understand it, but their cheeks grew still whiter and tears gathered in their eyes.

"What is it?" they cried. "What can it be?"

"The wounded are being taken away," explained Grandfather Willing solemnly. "Hark how the drivers hurry the horses! They are afraid! They are retreating! Thank God! Thank God!"

The storm drove the Willings indoors, but the sound followed them. Through the long afternoon, through the long night, the Willings heard

THE TERROR PAST

those wailing cries and those anguished commands to hasten.

When Sunday morning dawned, those cries were startling other farmhouses and villages miles away. They never faded entirely from the recollection of those who heard them.

Soon the boy from the next farmhouse crossed the fields again. The battle was over, the Northern arms were victorious, Gettysburg was safe.

"Now," said Grandmother Willing, "I want to go home."

Grandfather Willing pondered. He had been studying a route that he thought they could safely follow. He knew all the byroads and all the farmers' lanes across the fields.

"You stay here, mother. I wish you would stay here."

Grandmother Willing gave her

husband one look, and then lifted her cat, Tiger, into his basket.

In the mysterious dusky light of the Willing farmhouse, Emmeline and her brother Henry had stood for a long moment in one another's arms. They dared not accept with too much enthusiasm this sudden joy. The rain was beating on the roof and the windows. The delirious mutterings of the other inhabitants of the house had died away.

"O Emmeline!" said Henry again. "Little Emmeline, is it you?"

"Yes," said Emmeline, with a long sigh, "it is."

"How are they at home?"

"Mother is well, but Sister Bertha is sick."

"When did you come out here?"

THE TERROR PAST

"On Tuesday."

"Where," — Henry looked about, startled, — "where are grandfather and grandmother?"

"I imagine they went to Aunt Sally's."

"And you have been here *alone!*"

"No." Emmeline laughed feebly. "No, not alone."

Henry started again. Over his sister's shoulder he saw a man lying on the floor in the parlor.

"There are wounded men in this house!"

"Oh, yes!" said Emmeline.

"You have been taking care of these men!"

"I gave them water and biscuit, and I talked to them."

Henry went a step nearer the parlor door.

EMMELINE

"That man is — is dead, Emmeline! And you've been here alone!"

"I wasn't alone," protested Emmeline. Between her and yesterday, even between her and this morning, there was falling a haze, gray and concealing as the low-lying clouds outside. She began to weep. "There was some one here to take care of me. I have been safe all the time. And he is gone away forever!"

Henry looked into the parlor and the sitting-room, and then went upstairs. Emmeline heard him exclaim. When he came down again, he went to the kitchen door and looked out. The trampled fields were already sodden. At the foot of the garden was a trench, begun for a well and abandoned. It was not deep, but it was deep enough. There, shrouded in Grand-

THE TERROR PAST

mother Willing's comforters, were laid those who in this house had given their lives for their convictions. One of the Watson boys, coming to see how his neighbors had fared, saved Emmeline a share in the last sad ceremony of battle.

Presently night fell upon the little farmhouse. Henry and Emmeline slept side by side on Grandmother Willing's kitchen floor. Often Henry rose and went about the house to minister to the wounded in Grandmother Willing's beds. When he returned, he laid a protecting arm across his little sister and so fell asleep once more. The mystery of his release was now clear to him. The humanity of the act, the helplessness of his enemy, combined to create in his heart a bitter hatred of war, a hatred felt by all

EMMELINE

who had anything to do with that sad battlefield.

The broadening light of Sunday morning wakened brother and sister. Across the wide valley between the two battle lines, great wagons were traveling swiftly. For friend and foe alike doctors and nurses of the victorious army had begun their work of mercy. To the door of the Willing farmhouse came at noon an ambulance. Some houses the attendants had found deserted except for their suffering guests. In others were women who had performed incredible and uncounted deeds of mercy. Each house had its epic of heroism and danger and sorrow. A charm seemed to have been laid upon these heroic ministers; it was as if an angel standing before them had protected

THE TERROR PAST

them in their ways. Of them all, only one had perished.

In the Willing house there was little for doctors or nurses to do. The house was orderly once more; the surviving soldiers asked feebly about the result of the battle, and when they heard, turned their faces away even from Emmeline.

The homeward journey of Grandmother and Grandfather Willing ended in the middle of Sunday afternoon. It had been much more roundabout than Grandfather Willing had planned, more awful than he had dreamed. As they drew near the scene of battle and beheld on every side its sad destruction, their hearts failed them utterly. Where was Mary? How was poor Bertha? Where was Emmeline, Emmeline who was forever getting into mischief of some kind? Above all, where was Henry?

Grandmother Willing was thinking of him as they drew near the farmhouse. Then looking up, she saw him standing on the porch, and behind him, in the doorway, Emmeline. Grandmother Willing made no motion to alight from the wagon. She sat still with Tiger on her lap.

"How did *you* get here?" she asked in a trembling voice.

"We have been here all the time," said Emmeline. There came into the eyes of Emmeline a sudden sparkle. What a tale she had to tell Eliza Batterson!

Grandmother Willing allowed herself to be helped out of the carriage. She came rapidly through the gate and across the dooryard, which was

THE TERROR PAST

now trampled into a muddy slough. From the doorway she could see into her parlor with its stained carpet. She looked from it to the stains of the same color on her granddaughter's dress. In spite of all that Grandmother Willing had seen, she did not yet realize the full meaning of a battle.

"Has blood been shed here?" she asked in an awed tone.

With an arm round her, Henry said, "Yes, grandmother."

Grandmother Willing's gaze still rested upon Emmeline.

"Did you see this?" she demanded, as if Emmeline were to blame for having got herself once more into mischief. "Were you in the battle, Emmeline?"

"Yes."

"Did you have wounded rebels here?"

"Yes. There are some upstairs now!" cried Emmeline.

"In my house!" exclaimed Grandmother Willing. "In my beds!" Grandmother Willing's youthfulness was apparent in the speed with which she started up the stairs. "I'll 'rebel' them!"

Those below waited. They could trust her to do nothing violent.

"Oh, you poor, poor souls!" cried Grandmother Willing abovestairs.

An ambulance driver who was making a journey to Gettysburg now offered to take Henry and Emmeline home. Henry must join his company as soon as possible, and the best way to find them was to go to Gettysburg, where he could doubtless

Page 154

THE TERROR PAST

get information about their position. He was heavily oppressed by anxiety and alarm, and could hardly wait until the driver received his orders to start.

Along the wooded ridge the ambulance traveled; Henry sat in the seat with the driver, Emmeline in the body of the wagon. There was no road; they made their way round shattered cannon, wrecked caissons, and far sadder remnants of the great battle. They passed close by the seminary building, where the Union soldiers had first camped. It was five o'clock on Sunday afternoon, the most peaceful hour of the week; but Gettysburg's streets were thronged with soldiers, mounted and on foot. Citizens were on their doorsteps. This Sunday was a day not of rest, but of rejoicing.

EMMELINE

Suddenly Emmeline saw twinkling in the breeze before her a bit of color, and her pale cheeks flushed. From windows and doorposts floated once more Gettysburg's flag — the stars of white on a field of blue, the stripes of red and white.

Unobserved, Henry and Emmeline passed down the street. In the back of the wagon, Emmeline could not be seen, and as for Henry — no one looked twice at a Union soldier with a bandaged head. No one noticed them, in fact, until Mr. Bannon, who was sitting on his porch with his pipe, saw them; he lifted his arms with a shout and hurried forward in his lame way to greet them. He shouted some wild sentence at them, but they could not wait to be greeted by lame Mr. Bannon. Hand in hand

THE TERROR PAST

they went along the house and to the kitchen porch. There, at the open door, they paused.

"Well, mother," said Henry.

Mrs. Willing did not move. She was sitting by the opposite window shelling peas that had been planted, it seemed to her, a generation ago. She sat with a half-opened pod between her fingers and looked at her children. Mrs. Schmidt's brother, driving into town an hour ago from his farm beyond the battlefield, had reported the safety of his sister and her brood, but had brought no news of Emmeline. Mrs. Willing could not at first quite believe that here, in flesh and blood, were the two children who lay so heavily upon her heart.

"Is Bertha safe, mother?" asked Henry. Still Henry and Emmeline did not move, and Mrs. Willing did not rise to meet them.

"Yes," answered Mrs. Willing. "Bertha is asleep upstairs."

"Is——" began Henry, and then he repeated that single meaningless word. "Is——"

Now Emmeline had begun to move. She pursued, however, a strange course. She took a step toward her mother, then a step toward the corner of the room, then a step toward her mother, then another away from her mother. Mrs. Willing rose; the peas and their pods rolled in all directions.

"Mother!" cried Emmeline. "Mother! Mother!"

The first exclamation shocked Mrs. Willing. It was hoarse, and in its sharp tones was all the misery through which Emmeline had lived. The

THE TERROR PAST

second "Mother!" expressed pure astonishment and nothing else. But in the third was all Emmeline's youth restored.

Henry had seen the object toward which his sister's erratic steps were turned and had finished his sentence, "Is it mine, mother?" He now took his mother into his arms and put his head on her shoulder as if he himself were not a very long way from the cradle in which his son reposed.

But for Emmeline, tears were past. She knelt upon the floor, enchanted, enslaved, a happy servitor of the sister who, sleeping in her quiet bed, knew nothing of the new joy that awaited her.

"O mother!" cried Emmeline. "It *is* a baby!"

THE END

301 43

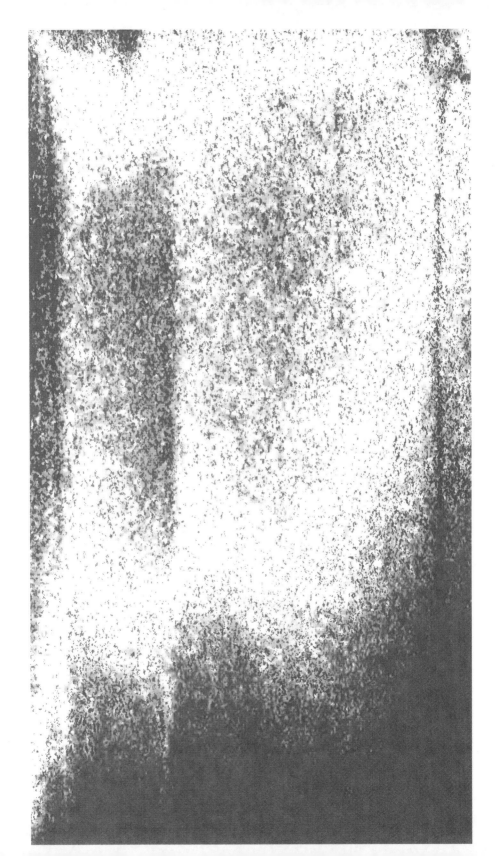

ImTheStory.com

Personalized Classic Books in many genre's

Unique gift for kids, partners, friends, colleagues

Customize:

- Character Names
- Upload your own front/back cover images (optional)
- Inscribe a personal message/dedication on the inside page (optional)

Customize many titles Including
- Alice in Wonderland
- Romeo and Juliet
- The Wizard of Oz
- A Christmas Carol
- Dracula
- Dr. Jekyll & Mr. Hyde
- And more...

CPSIA information can be obtained
at www.ICGtesting.com
Printed in the USA
LVOW10s0124190417
531319LV00032B/1546/P